A Place for Zero

A Math Adventure

Angeline Sparagna LoPresti

Illustrated by Phyllis Hornung

i📖i Charlesbridge

I dedicate this book to my husband Ernest, for being so supportive and helpful, and to my parents Philip and Isabelle Sparagna. — A.S.L.

For Grandma Hornung and Grandma Kieckers. — P.H.

Charlesbridge wishes to thank Stephanie Lim for her editorial contribution.

Text copyright ©2003 by Angeline Sparagna LoPresti

Illustrations copyright ©2003 by Phyllis Hornung

Published by Charlesbridge, 85 Main Street, Watertown, MA 02472

617.926.0329 • www.charlesbridge.com

Printed by Sung In Printing in Gunpo-Si, Kyonggi-Do, Korea

(hc) 10 9 8 7 6 5   (sc) 20 19 18 17 16

Library of Congress Cataloging-in-Publication Data
LoPresti, Angeline Sparagna.
  A place for Zero : a math adventure / by Angeline Sparagna LoPresti ; illustrated by Phyllis Hornung.
  p. cm.
  Summary: As Zero searches to find his place, he learns of his additive and multiplicative identities, and then he establishes place value.
  ISBN 978-1-57091-602-1 (reinforced for library use)   ISBN 978-1-57091-196-5 (softcover)   ISBN 978-1-60734-158-1 (ebook pdf)
  1. Zero (The number)—Juvenile literature. [1. Zero (The number) 2. Number concept.] I. Hornung, Phyllis, ill. II. Title.
QA141.3 .L76 2002
513—dc21
                                                                                              2002002412

Not long ago, Zero lay floating on the calm waters of Central Lake. He could hear the happy cries of the other numbers, 1 through 9, as they played in the meadow. Zero didn't play Addemup because he had nothing to add. He felt he had no place among the other digits.

Zero lived in Digitaria, a curious country ruled by King Multiplus and Queen Addeleine. Their positive outlook helped the kingdom prosper.

Count Infinity, the King's trusted advisor, was the one who shaped all the numbers. When old digits retired, he replaced them with shiny new numerals.

Every number knew its place. A 7 was the number of days in a week, and a 5 was the number of points on a star. A 2 was handy for counting the wheels on a bicycle.

The 1s were important because Count Infinity added them together to make the other numbers.

Every number had a place except Zero. Count Infinity had been experimenting when he formed the strange new digit. But Zero meant nothing, and no one was sure what his job would be. King Multiplus declared that no more zeros would be made until they found a purpose for this one.

Zero was alone.

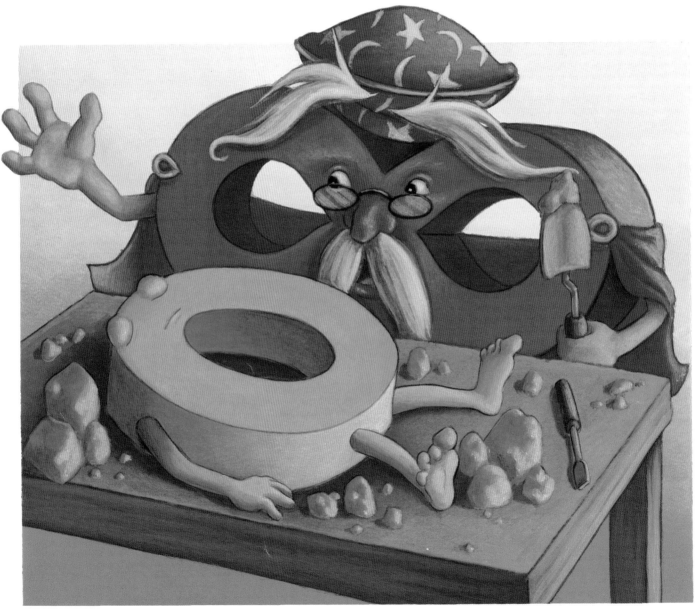

Nowadays no one mentioned Zero much.
The few times someone tried to count with him,
they always ended up with nothing.

"I need to find my place," Zero thought.
He decided to go back to visit the wise old
Count Infinity and ask his advice.

Count Infinity made incredible things. He made knickknacks, whatsits, and thingamajigs. The most impressive thing he ever made was an enormous machine: the Numberator. The Numberator had a vacuum tube on one side and a large curved spout on the other.

When Count Infinity placed digits under the tube, they were sucked up with a great clanking and whirring until, finally, they emerged from the spout — with a totally new number. Count Infinity could put in two ones to make a bouncy baby two or three ones to make a roly-poly little three.

9

As Zero stood shyly in the doorway, Count Infinity looked up and noticed him.

"Ah, young Zero!" Infinity exclaimed. "You're just in time to help me figure out a better way to make a 1."

"What do you mean?" Zero asked.

"Well, most numbers are easy to make. I simply pop a handful of 1s into my trusty Numberator. Making a 1, though — that's trickier."

"To make a 1," Count Infinity explained, "I spend hours handcrafting it from a special material called integrium."

"Why don't you just stick one 1 into the Numberator?" Zero asked.

Count Infinity sighed. "I've tried that, but the Numberator adds. You have to put in at least two numbers. No two numbers that I can think of add up to —"

Count Infinity eyed Zero in a strange way.

"Could you put this 1 into the Numberator for me?" the Count asked. "Just help the 1 stand right under the vacuum tube . . ."

As Zero did, he was sucked up into the Numberator along with the 1!

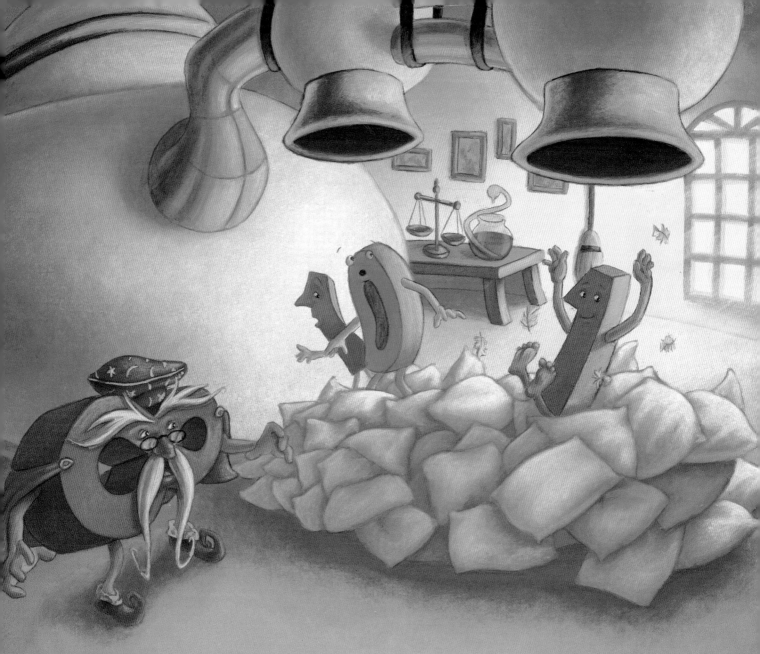

Zero barely had time to realize what was happening before he was out the other side. Sitting next to him were the old 1 and a shiny new 1.

"Wonderful!" Count Infinity cried. "We have discovered your additive identity. I bet my binomials that if we add you to any number, we will always come up with the same number. You can help replenish the supply of digits in Digitaria!"

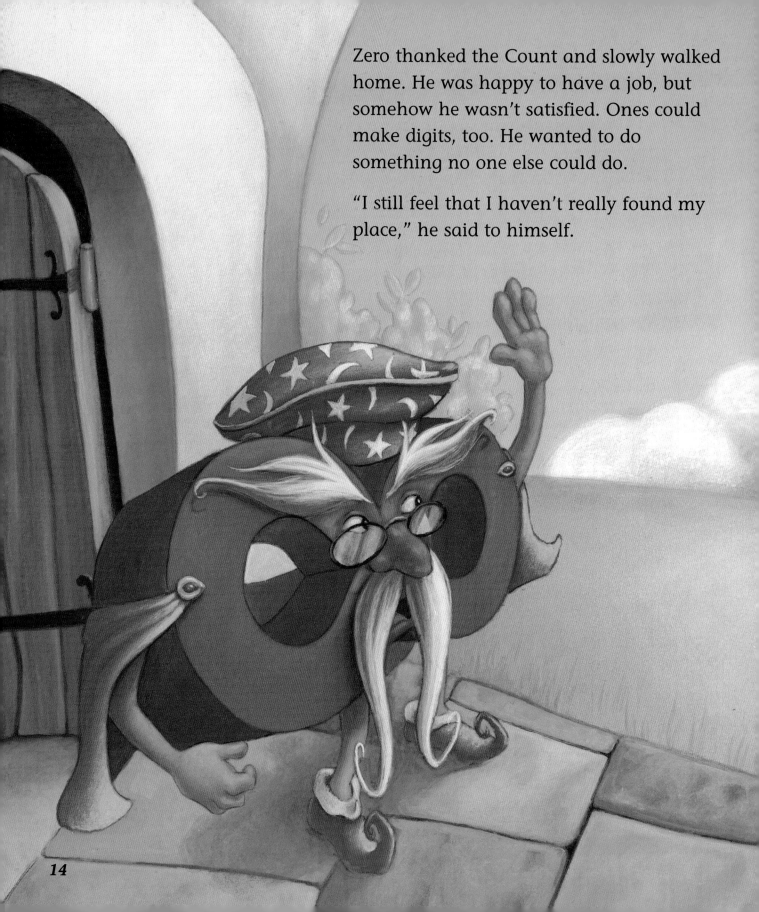

Zero thanked the Count and slowly walked home. He was happy to have a job, but somehow he wasn't satisfied. Ones could make digits, too. He wanted to do something no one else could do.

"I still feel that I haven't really found my place," he said to himself.

As Zero walked, he had an idea: "I wonder what would happen if I were multiplied with another number?"

Everyone knew that multiplication was a powerful thing, and only the King could use it. Often the product of the multiplied numbers would be too large for anyone to understand.

Zero swallowed hard at the boldness of his idea. Then he stood up as straight as a round digit can. "I will ask the King," he decided, and set off for the castle.

At the gates of the castle, Zero was stopped by two sharp-looking 7s.

"What kind of number are you?" one guard asked. "You look like a 9 someone squished." Both guards began to laugh.

"I need to ask the King about multiplication," said Zero.

The guards stopped laughing. They looked at each other. "W-well," said one, "you'd better go right in."

Zero entered the castle. He saw King Multiplus and Queen Addeleine on their thrones. Crowds of numbers filled the hall, waiting to address them. The 5 standing next to Zero asked why he was there.

"I'm asking the King to multiply me," Zero answered.

The 5 gasped. Other numbers who heard began to whisper.

"Absolute nine-sense!"

"It's two much!"

Soon a loud buzz rippled through the hall.

"What is the meaning of this?" King Multiplus boomed, displeased by the growing confusion.

"It's Zero," Queen Addeleine told him. "And something about multiplication."

"Multiplication!" the King exclaimed. "That is serious business. Let him come forward and explain himself."

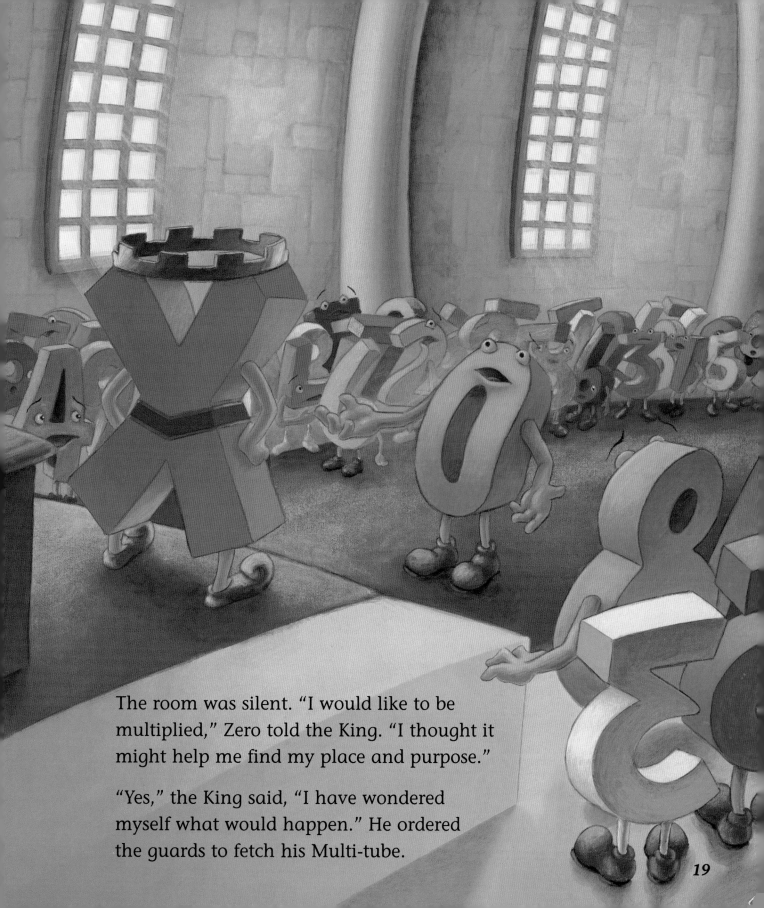

The room was silent. "I would like to be multiplied," Zero told the King. "I thought it might help me find my place and purpose."

"Yes," the King said, "I have wondered myself what would happen." He ordered the guards to fetch his Multi-tube.

The tube was made of solid integrium.

"We need to find someone who is willing to be multiplied with Zero," the King said. No one moved. Finally, a young 1 stepped forward.

"I'll do it," the 1 said bravely. Together Zero and the 1 jumped into the "FACTOR" end of the tube.

All that could be heard was the clanking
and whirring of the tube.

Suddenly, Zero and the 1 shot out of the other end of the tube. As Zero looked around, he saw beside him a small, round figure who looked strangely familiar.

"Five alive!" exclaimed the King. "It's another zero!"

The other numbers were speechless.

"Why, we must try this again," declared the flabbergasted King. "This time, we will multiply Zero with a 7." He called for one of his 7 guards. The guard's knees shook as he stepped forward.

The same thing happened with Zero and the 7. The King laughed and said, "Well, Zero, you have your answer. No matter what number we multiply you with, we get zero!"

This was big news. The other numbers chattered excitedly, but Zero said, "Now there are more zeros with no real place."

The 1 patted Zero on the back. Zero was glad to have a friend at a time like this.

"I want to make new numbers that no one has ever seen before," Zero said. "Sire, what number do you get if you add 1 to 9?"

It was one of those questions that no one ever asked. The King coughed. "As everyone knows, anything bigger than 9 is *many*," he said. "We don't think about 1 plus 9 because there is no digit for a number that big."

Zero looked at the 1 standing next to him. He rubbed his eyes. Together, he and the 1 looked like this: 10.

"Sire!" he cried. "Look at us! We can make a new number to represent what you get when you add 1 and 9."

The King scratched his chin.

Zero asked nine 1s to stand together. "Sire, if we added one more to this group, we could use a 0 to show that all those 1s have moved over to the next place. When I stand in this place, next to my friend 1, as a zero I can represent zero 1s. But he now represents 9 + 1."

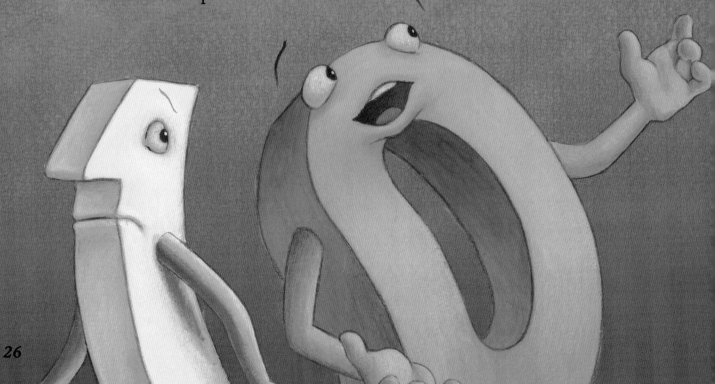

"I like your thinking, Zero," the King said. "But," he whispered, "I can't call the new number *9 + 1*. Quick, think of a new name!"

Zero whispered back, "This new number will attend to a lot of business. Could we call it *Attend*?"

The King couldn't hear Zero very well, so in a loud voice he said, "I proclaim that this new number will be called a TEN!"

The numbers all loved it.
"Hooray for TEN! Hooray for TEN!" they cheered.

The numbers crowded around Zero and asked if they could
stand beside him. Zero gave each digit a turn and soon they
were making wonderful new numbers like 20, 30, 60, and 90.

Before long they were standing next to each other in different combinations, to make all kinds of new numbers: 32, 47, 89, and on and on. Big numbers didn't seem quite so scary anymore.

When the excitement calmed down, Zero felt someone tugging at his arm. "What about me?" asked a small voice.

"Is it my turn to stand next to you?" the new little 0 asked.

"I'm sorry," Zero said. "Two 0s standing next to each other still equal nothing." The little 0 looked so sad that the brave 1 and Zero each put an arm around her. Suddenly, Zero had a thought. "Look, sire!" he called to the King. "What do we look like?"

The King said slowly, "Why, you look like a new number, bigger than any I've ever seen. Bigger even than the new number 90."

Zero said proudly, "We can represent what you get when you have ten 10s."

"Splendid!" exclaimed the King.

Soon, all the other digits were clamoring to stand next to the two 0s. They made numbers like 500 and 700. A 9 got so excited when he helped make the number 900 that he almost fell over.

In the middle of the excitement, Zero noticed Count Infinity beaming at him.

"Well, Zero," the Count smiled, "did you find what you were looking for?"

Zero nodded. "I just wanted to mean more than nothing," he said. "And now I think I've finally found my place."

From then on, Zero played Addemup
as happily as everyone else.